WOMEN AT PRAYER

The Madeleva Lecture in Spirituality

This series, sponsored by the Center for Spirituality, Saint Mary's College, Notre Dame, Indiana, honors annually the woman who as president of the college inaugurated its pioneering program in theology, Sister M. Madeleva, C.S.C.

1985
Monika K. Hellwig
Christian Women in a Troubled World

1986
Sandra M. Schneiders
Women and the Word

WOMEN AT PRAYER

MARY COLLINS

1987 Madeleva Lecture
in Spirituality

PAULIST PRESS
New York/Mahwah

Library of Congress Cataloging-in-Publication Data

Collins, Mary, 1935–
    Women at prayer.

    "1987 Madeleva lecture in spirituality."
    Bibliography: p.
    I. Women—Religious life.   2. Prayer.   I. Title.
II. Title: Madeleva lecture in spirituality.
BX2353.C59   1987   248.3'088042   87–7240
ISBN 0-8091-2949-3 (pbk.)

Published by Paulist Press
997 Macarthur Blvd.
Mahwah, N.J. 07430

Printed and bound in the United States of America

WOMEN AT PRAYER

WOMEN'S HERITAGE

The matter of women at prayer seems a commonplace Catholic concern. We have many images of women praying: older women in parish churches, elderly nuns in convent chapels, mothers with their children at bedtime, wives with their husbands. We have models: Mary the Mother of Jesus (Lk 1:46–55), Miriam the prophetess of the exodus leading the women in praise (Ex 15:20–21), Judith and Esther interceding for their people (Jdt 9:2–14; Est C: 14–30), the Canaanite woman asking Jesus to help her sick daughter (Mt 15:21–28), the woman before the unjust judge in the gospel parable (Lk 18:1–7), Scholastica, who prayed to God and was heard when her brother Benedict refused her request.[1] We have some mentors, women who have walked the path of prayer, who have been able to report to us what we might expect to meet on our way, and who have encouraged us to set out ourselves: Catherine of Siena and Teresa of Avila, both named doctors—that is, teachers—of the church in our day by Pope Paul VI, Julian of Norwich, Gertrude of Helfta, Mechtilde of Magdeburg, Hildegard of Bingen, Thérèse of Lisieux.[2]

We have an enviable richness in our Catholic tradition. And in this late twentieth century, we are the beneficiaries of two movements which have brought this heritage of women at prayer closer to us. The first is a widespread revival of interest in the life of prayer. The second is the women's movement, with its concern to reclaim and to value the too-long-forgotten and too-easily-deprecated contributions of women to human history. These two movements have created the demand for books of writings about prayer, including women's writings. We have an unprecedented number of studies going on related to women's spirituality and women's experiences in prayer.[3]

The studies have not only confirmed the abundance of spiritual riches that have come to the world through women at prayer. They have also raised difficult questions for the Christian churches to look at. We might summarize the matter in two points. First, we are becoming newly aware that women gifted in prayer faced sizable obstacles when they wanted to communicate their experiences of God to the church. Second, we know now that these Christian women with deep prayer lives regularly faced suspicion and even outright hostility; if their gifts were not suppressed, they were inevitably marginalized, never allowed to influence the public tradition of the church's prayer. We can wonder what spiritual insight and power was lost because of these circumstances.

The obstacles our sisters faced in communicating their experiences of God came in at least two forms: deprivation and dismissal. Because women seldom had access to adequate educations, with rare exceptions they lacked the literary, the critical, and the artistic skills to write confidently of their experiences. They were often truly at a loss for words.

Even after women's experiences of God in prayer were adequately recorded, their contributions too seldom received a receptive hearing in the forums where educated medieval churchmen reflected on the human experience of the mystery of God. In monastery schools, cathedral closes, and the young and vigorous medieval universities the truth and worth of women's experience of God was not even an interesting question. Instead, individual clerics serving as confessors to holy women scrutinized and judged what women revealed to them about their life of prayer. The woman who entertained and persisted in untraditional visions and thoughts was subject to ridicule as a crazy woman or an hysterical one; she might be accused of being in collu-

3

sion with demons; she might be detained and punished by the Inquisition.[4]

Church censors quite readily suppressed women's original accounts of their life of prayer. Occasionally sympathetic churchmen helped to edit a holy woman's writing for "correctness." This male scrutiny and judgment of women's experiences at prayer deprived too many women of their own spiritual judgment. When women's experiences of God were blocked in this way God's continuing self-disclosure within the church was thwarted.

Even if a woman's account of her experiences of God survived ecclesiastical scrutiny and censorship, the church paid little attention to what she had to say. No one expected much of women or from them. Thomas Aquinas expressed the prevailing viewpoint when he noted that women, passive by nature, are incapable of expressing eminence and so are unsuited for any leadership.[5] One story, that of the rise of devotion to the Sacred Heart followed by the designation of a liturgical feast, illustrates the characteristic way in which the church responded to women's experiences of God in prayer.

We find the image of the Sacred Heart of Jesus as an object of Christian devotion developed in an integrated form in the twelfth century in Gertrude the Great's *Revelation of Divine Love*.[6]

The revelation remained private, shared only with the few who read Gertrude's writings, until the Carthusian monks of Cologne began to promote the image in the fifteenth century, in a crassly physical iconography still familiar in popular devotion. In the seventeenth century, Margaret Mary Alacoque's rich spirituality was centered in her experience of the love of the Sacred Heart of Jesus. But it was John Eudes who was able to get official ecclesiastical approbation for public devotion to the Sacred Heart. That popular devotion got a liturgical foothold only in the eighteenth century, through the effort of Polish Carmelite priests and the Polish hierarchy. Only in the twentieth century did this revelation of divine love in the Sacred Heart of Jesus become a feast of the universal church, and only after repeated efforts to purify the image of its more crass popular features.[7]

In retrospect, it is evident upon a simple rereading that Gertrude of Helfta's revelation had risen out of her liturgical experience and was fully integrated with it. It took churchmen eight centuries to negotiate—first to elaborate, and then to refine to their satisfaction—the image of loving presence that God had revealed to Gertrude as a gift to the church. A story such as this alerts us to the likelihood that the liturgical and devotional life of the church has suffered many such deprivations because women's experiences of divine presence and blessing were dismissed or marginalized.

WOMEN'S IMAGINATION

Interesting as this rich heritage is, I am not going to center on women of earlier centuries and their experiences of God in prayer. I propose to set out in another direction, looking at three individual women of our own day, each self-identified with the Catholic tradition, and one group of thirteen Jewish women, whose experiences of the living God invite us into the deep center of reality. There is risk in this adventure, because my choice of mentors for contemporary women at prayer carries with it the full absence of ecclesiastical approbation. Furthermore, I have not chosen women who are generally thought of as holy women—interesting, perhaps, but not holy. Neither have I chosen women who will be recognized as institutionally identified churchwomen. Dorothy Day is not on my list, nor the four women martyrs of El Salvador. But I have chosen women who are unashamed God-seekers and who have not been afraid to trust and to give imaginative expression to their experiences of God in this late twentieth century western culture. And I have chosen women with gifts for communicating their experiences. They are poets, painters, and writers, women skilled in the use of line and color, rhythms and words. They would hardly call themselves mystics, but I venture to call them by that name. They have gone beyond form and the familiar, and have returned to tell us about the truth of God.

My list of exemplars of contemporary women at prayer includes the writer Annie Dillard, the poet Anne Sexton, and the painter Meinrad Craighead. Complementing these individuals is the group of women who gather at the imaginative center they name "Miriam's well."

On what grounds and by what authority did I choose them? Years ago I let myself be convinced by the poet T. S. Eliot that our humankind cannot bear too much reality, and I consider that truth axiomatic. It is the artists, the poets, and the mystics among us who venture outside the enclosed structures of the familiar world to explore the unknown. They go to inner places to which they give names like "the edge of the rim" of reality or "edge of the central opening" and "Miriam's well."[8] Or they liken the inward journey to a polar expedition, where all the baggage of social existence is abandoned piece by piece as the stripped explorer approaches closer and closer to the mysterious pole.[9]

We might wonder whether mystical exploration becomes contemporary women who are finding their way in the modern world. Ample evidence exists that women of other times and cultures have gone to "the edge of the rim" in their quest for God. Wise women who have studied the history of women's spirituality are now counseling this generation of women to be contemplatives. Inner groans at this news will register as the legitimate response of women who are already struggling with so many other expectations. There seems to be no limit to what is being called forth from the educated, integrated total woman. Being contemplative ought certainly to be optional! Yet there are serious reasons why developing a contemplative spirit is an imperative for women. To state it baldly, God needs contemplative women, the church of Jesus Christ needs them, and the welfare of the human race and the planet requires it. We need to explore those claims and their implications.

In the 1986 Madeleva lecture Sandra Schneiders observed that it is the imagination which governs our experience of God because the imagination creates our God-image and our self-image.[10] In the light of that truth she warned that our religious imaginations must be healed of wounds inflicted on men and women alike by the distorted males-only image of a patriarchal God. She called for a therapy of the imagination, noting that such therapy is an affair of language, broadly understood. She further asserted that we must stop trivializing the issue and begin the long process of conversion to worship of the living and true God. But how do we begin?

In my judgment, we must consult the imaginatively gifted, who may have the resources for healing the psychic damage which is blocking living faith. But we also need to recognize that the religiously, imaginatively gifted have always been among us. The new question is how we can bring their fuller imaging of God into the tradition of the public prayer of the church. The step from personal insight to expressive form is fundamental; the artist takes this step alone. The further movement from the fashioning of healing images to their incorporation into the liturgical tradition is decisive. It is the more difficult step to negotiate.[11]

LECTIO DIVINA:
THROUGH WORDS TO GOD

Creative contemplative feminists, whether they seek God on the mystical or the liturgical path, are women who are willing to welcome and trust their own experiences of God. Before we consult them, however, we must situate their activity in the larger context of the church's tradition of contemplative prayer. My account of this is deliberately detailed, in order to suggest the power of biblical language to shape religious experience.

Benedictines, following the monastic sources grounded in the tradition of the desert mothers and fathers, the holy *ammas* and *abbas*, named the way of prayer *lectio divina*, sacred reading. It was a "journey through words, up the path of speech, on toward God."[12]

Ordinarily, the text to be read in *lectio divina* is the scripture.[13] For the ancients, reading the text was first of all a matter of literacy, of knowing how to read anything at all. Knowing how to read goes beyond word recognition to comprehension of meaning. Teachers of reading know that children can learn to say strings of individual words without ever catching on to how written language works. Reading the sacred text well— getting its point—is the first moment in *lectio divina* as a way of prayer.

The second moment in the tradition of *lectio divina* involves meditating on the text. Meditating for the ancients meant vigorous physical activity. They wanted the text to become flesh in them, and without any sophisticated biological appreciation of the formation of neural traces in the brain, they had an intuition that taking in the written text meant physical engagement with the words. The ancients read important texts aloud over and over, forming each word with their lips, using their vocal cords, hearing the words address them in their own ears so that they might penetrate to what St. Benedict called "the ear of the heart."

Some of the ancients likened the second step, learning the text by heart or taking it to heart, to a cow chewing her cud. The cow takes her feed in, brings it to the first chamber of her four-chambered stomach, reserves it there for slow mastication, savors what she ruminates, and in this slow process of letting the food pass from the one chamber to the next gets fully nourished. Christians at prayer do not have four-chambered stomachs, but they have both an outer and an inner ear. It is the ear of the heart which must be nourished. Savoring the images and symbols of the text, walking into the world that the text opens up to the human imagination, meditators can begin to see and to hear good news embodied in the biblical text. Alternately, they can see and hear a message which distresses them, which causes a kind of spiritual indigestion.

The third movement in *lectio divina* was named *oratio,* praying. It involves making a personal response to the words spoken to the ear of the heart, to the vision shown to the inner eye of the imagination. If *meditatio* might be characterized as God's addressing of human hearts through the mind and the imagination, *oratio* names the human part of the dialogue. God's address heard with the ear of the heart might evoke joy or remorse, perhaps grief, perhaps gratitude. In the biblical tradition, *oratio* might even evoke struggle with God. A serious pray-er might respond to the biblical word by quarreling with the one whose reportedly steadfast love is shown in curiously unloving ways.

The fourth movement is what the ancient monastics called *contemplatio,* delighting in the divine presence, a resting in the heart of God that goes beyond dialogue, a wordless awareness that beyond all the words was the true gift. *Contemplatio* meant enjoying the reality of God's love, abandoning all fear, drawing near, and trusting God's mysterious wisdom or incomprehensible purpose in human lives. All of the other movements of the way of *lectio divina* are meant to lead to these moments of pure and simple prayer, these attitudes of loving and trusting hearts. We often reserve the name mystic for those persons who have walked the full length of the path of prayer, beyond the images to the living God.

But the path of *lectio divina* begins with words and images even if it leads beyond them. The principal resource for images to open us up to the experience of God in this traditional way of contemplative prayer is the bible. The God-seeker who takes up the biblical narrative and biblical poetry as a spiritual source is brought into regular contact with the God of Abraham, Isaac, and Jacob, the God of the patriarchs and proph-

12

ets, the God who acts as king, lord, warrior, judge. The God of the biblical narrative is the same one who is the Father of our Lord Jesus Christ, God's only-begotten and well-beloved Son. The God of the biblical narrative and most biblical poetry seems to show a male face and to be surrounded by male devotees worshiping and serving him. Women in this resource seem to hover at the margins of every human meeting with God.

The image world opened up for people who follow the traditional way of biblical prayer is a patriarchal, androcentric world. The words spoken to the ear of the human heart and the vision set before the inner eye seem the script of a redemptive drama with a males-only cast for the dramatic roles, with just a few women playing bit parts and walk-through roles.

The church's biblical renewal, the renewal of prayer, the liturgical renewal and the women's movement have been occurring simultaneously in our culture. After two decades, some significant testimony is gathering from this religious and cultural convergence. Some women who have been feeding their spirits with this food of the biblical word of God report that no matter how faithfully they come to this scriptural table they are being malnourished. Praying the bible devotedly and listening to the treasures of scripture being proclaimed in the liturgical assembly, they have unexpectedly begun either to doubt their own significance before God or to doubt that the God of the bible is significant for their spiritual well-being. Some of the most sensitive can no longer stomach the biblical word, refuse it, and are looking for other sources of spiritual nourishment. Some have internalized as the word of God a word saying that God intends them to be marginal and subservient and are letting it become flesh in their lives.

In this regard Monica Furlong makes some important observations on the role the church plays in the life of prayer.[14] She notes that we regularly talk and act as though the purpose of the church is to put people directly in touch with God. On the surface of things, that presumption is correct. The church claims that its book, the bible, prayed in *lectio divina* and proclaimed in the liturgy, is a record of God's self-revelation and of fully human responses to God. But Furlong alerts us that the church plays an opposite, protective role, too. She argues that in its mediatorial role the church tries to "filter out" experiences of God that might be "overwhelming." Later, we will return to the matter of our being overwhelmed by the living God. Here it is enough to note Furlong's judgment that unless we are given safe approaches some of us would live lives devoid of any deep inner experience and others of us might get drawn into mystical experiences so powerful that they threaten sanity.

Nevertheless, while the church forms our common religious imagination through the images and narratives of scripture, our feminist sisters are telling us that false approaches to God through the distorting filters of androcentrism and patriarchy are killing the spirits of some of our contemporaries. The rest of us risk living distorted and alienated lives. God-seeking women will have limited freedom to enjoy the divine presence and to risk the divine embrace when the path of biblical prayer initially leads women into a world of estranging images. What can women do?

FOLKLORE: THE PATH OF WISDOM TOWARD GOD

Earlier I mentioned the group of Jewish women who have begun to gather around an imaginative center they have named "Miriam's well." They are prototypes of the many Jewish and Christian women who assemble in faith, confident that the living God to whom they pray is greater than the patriarchal images that biblical religion has recorded in its sacred texts.[15] There are, they note, two other texts of divine revelation whose reading has been neglected too long. The first is the text of women's lives in their own bodies. The second is the story of the women who were participants in the revelatory events described in the bible but whose accounts of their experiences were never recorded. They believe that each text—the text of their lives, the stories of women involved in the beginnings, and the biblical narrative—is a source for the correct interpretation of the other. All three must be read together.

This "reading" takes place on the day the Jewish calendar calls Rosh Hodesh, the "head of the month," the day of the new moon, an acknowledgment that the cosmic rhythms of the moon are repeated in the biological rhythms of women's lives. Rosh Hodesh invites women to celebrate the mystery of God revealed in women's and cosmic mysteries. The long-overlooked text of women's wisdom is called "the text of the month."

Why call it a text at all? Perhaps because biblical religion—Jewish and also Christian—is so firmly grounded in an understanding that God speaks a living and life-giving word, a word which must be heard with the ear of the heart. According to this thinking, the text of the month embodied in women, embedded in the cosmos, is an unwritten word, but a word of God nonetheless.

Folklore is always about truth, truth expressed in story form. Jewish folklore remembers what the bible does not record, that every male tribal ancestor had a twin sister; the youngest of the brothers, Benjamin, was the one male among triplets.[16] The thirteen sisters' existence is documented in the thirteen moons of the religious calendar. The women gathering at Miriam's well have wondered: What if the women of Israel had written a second Torah scroll, writing down teaching nowhere else recorded? Or what if God had entrusted to Miriam, the prophetess of the exodus and the midwife of the birth of the people of God, the teaching for this yet-to-be-written scroll, just as he had given Moses the teaching for the two tablets of the law?

The folkloric memory and contemporary musings about it provide the context for the monthly gathering at Miriam's well to read the text of the month. But folklore has important content as well to contribute to women's ritual gatherings in the name of biblical religion. There is the matter of Miriam's song. Scholars tell us that Miriam's song is the oldest recorded fragment of direct human speech responding to the wonder God worked at the Red Sea. We read:

> Miriam the prophetess . . . took a timbrel in her hand, and all the women went out after her with timbrels and dances. And Miriam answered them: "Sing to the Lord; for he

has triumphed gloriously; the horse and his
rider has he thrown into the sea" (Ex 15:20).

But Miriam's song is unfinished, according to the
commentators, so that future generations will
take up and complete the singing and dancing
begun long ago in the Egyptian desert. The tradition remains open; that is the message of Miriam's unfinished song.

So also, the folkloric tradition remembers,
the guardianship of the desert well-spring was
entrusted to Miriam.[17] The desert well was itself
a manifestation of God's gathering of the waters
into a basin on the second day of creation. From
the beginning these waters had been entrusted to
women, who were themselves shaped as vessels,
made as keepers of the waters of life. Because
Miriam was wise about the ways of waters—the
waters of the womb when she had been a midwife, the waters of the Nile on whose banks she
hid the infant Moses, the waters of the Red Sea—
the well was given to Miriam to care for.

Miriam's well names for these Jewish women
the center—or "the edge of the central opening"—to which God draws them as women. The
place is "a place of darkness where something important is hidden." It is "a womb deep, full, and
endless, the womb of the imagination," or "a
place where tears collect." It is a place where
many women come—some without cup or

bucket—for refreshment and find hospitality. It is "a place around which to dance life's dances" and a "source of songs that our mothers sang before us."[18]

The gatherings at Miriam's well each month bring together the month of the religious tradition, the month of the earth's turning, and the month of women's lives. If it is March–April, the month is Nisan, the month of the Passover, the month of springtime, the month of Miriam's deeds, the month of bondage and freedom played out not only in history but also in women's lives. If it is November–December, the month of Kislev and the feast of Hanukkah, it is the month of Judith and Deborah, the month of women's courage, the month to celebrate women as light within darkness.

In the groups of women who seek the presence of God in these monthly celebrations, someone is named "keeper" of the month, the guardian of its wisdom. This woman guides the group to explore the familiar traditions in new ways, to wonder "what if . . ."—to reach deeper into Miriam's well. Keeping the month involves tying the biblical tradition to God's truth manifest in themselves as women; it means giving expression to truths spoken by God a long time past but hardly heard or almost forgotten. Forgotten stories are remembered; forgotten women's lives are rediscovered; forgotten or unnoticed images of God's presence are now recognized for what they are. Miriam's well, finally, is not meant to be a secret place reserved exclusively for women, but a place of refreshment for a parched, thirsty, dehydrated humanity lost wandering in a desert of its own making. But women are the first to gather at Miriam's well. They plunge into their imaginations, anchored by their own bodies and biblical religion, to learn who they are and who God is.

What images have the God-seekers at Miriam's well drawn forth? The well itself, the moon, water and vessel, womb, earth, tree and flame, are prominent on the list. When we reflect we see that these are symbolic forms arising from experienced "facts," cosmic, biological, and cultural facts.[19] The moon, the water, the tree, and the soil of earth are realities of the cosmos and this planet. The womb is a biological reality. The well, the flame, and the vessel are domestic cultural forms, manifestations of human creativity for which women have cared in every society. In Judaism, the lighting of household lamps and cooking fires remains a religious act even in a technological era.

Interestingly, the cultural, the biological, and the cosmic forms interpret one another in this collection of images. A well, a womb, and a vessel contain dark interior spaces. So also the soil of earth is full of dark burrows, holes, and hidden recesses. Wells, wombs, vessels—each holds the waters of life.

The flame and the moon bring light into darkness; they grow and recede in brilliance, each in its own time. The planet's waters and the waters of the womb both repond to the pull of the moon. The tree and the human body are similar in form—roots holding to the earth, trunk and branches reaching upward. The human female like the tree has vital sap flowing through her and out of her—water and blood and milk—nurturing life and purifying itself. Her body yields fruit in due time.[20]

Are these images adequate bearers of revelation about the mystery of God? Can these symbolic forms become vital sacraments of God's presence in the church's liturgical assemblies? Can stories of God be told around them? Will they tell of the God of biblical religion or of a foreign god? Will these new stories allow as-yet-unrecognized aspects of the covenant God YHWH to break through into the church's conscious experience? That is the exploration feminist liturgists are doing wherever they gather in faith. They are engaged in serious play, play similar to the playing the child does to learn about the outer world, trying to grasp its basic relationships.[21] Unlike the child, feminist liturgists, Jewish and Christian, are capable of reflecting on the bearing of these explorations for the integrity of the religious traditions.

Feminist liturgists collaborate in their explorations, since liturgy is by definition the ritual symbolic act of an assembly. The feminist contemplative who is also an artist explores and creates in solitude. Meinrad Craighead spent fourteen years of her adult life in the English Stanbrook Abbey as a Benedictine contemplative nun. Her formal daily prayer there, the divine office and the Eucharist, would have presented to her listening heart year after year the full range of the biblical story of redemption. This public praying of the official prayer of the church with her sisters would have been integrated through the contemplative journey inward. We might assume that this journey would have followed the traditional path of *lectio divina* had she not released for our viewing a collection of forty paintings with brief commentary entitled *The Mother's Songs* and subtitled "Images of God the Mother."

From her introduction we learn that these images had been growing within her long before she went to the Benedictine abbey. She writes,

22

"God the Mother came to me when I was a child, and as children will do, I kept her a secret. We hid together inside the structures of institutional Catholicism." The hiding took place, she says, at her inmost center. On the surface of things she was comfortably Catholic. "My Catholic heritage and environment," she observes, "have been like a beautiful river flowing over my subterranean foundation in God the Mother. The two movements are not in conflict, they simply water different layers in my soul."[22]

She credits her maternal grandmother and her mother as the source of the stories that awakened the images of God the Mother. The result of her inner grounding in this image world was a profound sense of security and stability. Her creativity as an artist she views as a handing on to others the gift that was given to her. "Contemplatio aliis tradere" was the way the medievals expressed it: handing on to others the fruits of one's contemplation.

What forms tell this contemplative woman of the presence of God the Mother? Many of the cosmic, biological, and cultural forms found at Miriam's well recur in Meinrad Craighead's painting. Dark interior recesses—holes in the earth, earthenware vessels, the dark recesses of the womb, hollowed trunks of ancient trees, pools and springs of water—contain the mystery.

Recalling her childhood impulse to bury all

the dead things she came upon—small animals like birds and rabbits and frogs, but also dead roses, hen feathers and discarded bones—she recognizes it now as an act of worship. "The Mother is abysmal space. A hole, the hollow is hallowed, and hallowed, it heals. Here the holy dead are seed in her dark matrix, take root, and are re-membered."[23] The holy mystery whose face she is seeking is life itself. It is hidden not only in the dead but also in seeds and eggs, and in the blood, milk, and water welling in the dark recesses of reality.

The contemplative artist calls New Mexico, where she now lives, "the land which matched my interior landscape." When she first visited the place in 1960, "What my eyes saw meshed with images I carried inside my body. Pictures painted on the walls of my womb began to emerge." In her collection she offers us God the Mother manifest in the Hopi kiva, the sacred hole in the ground into whose fruitful recesses the devotee descends.[24] Feeling the desert and mountain winds, what the Native Americans call "Old Wind Woman," she recognized and painted God the Mother inhaling and exhaling, expanding and contracting, encircling, encoiling and recoiling, spiraling, "her spirit evolving, involving the entire universe."[25]

Color, line, and form cannot be reduced to language. "Images of God the Mother" must be seen with the eye for their truth to be recognized. But they are the kind of as yet unwritten and uncelebrated "text" of God's self-disclosure to women that the women at Miriam's well were looking for, these "pictures painted on the wall of the womb."

That image of womb paintings suggests what I believe may be the most important recovery Craighead's work offers toward the healing of human imaginations. Her collection opens with a painting of a girl of ten and a dog prone on the ground gazing into each other's eyes. As she recalls the moment, it signals the start of her conscious search for the face of God and her intuitive recognition that she would "never travel further than into this animal's eyes."[26]

Seeking the face of God in the created world has been a small part of biblical religion; it is an insignificant part of public worship in the Christian churches.[27] Feminist theologian Rosemary Ruether suggests an explanation for this fact when she notes that the Christian tradition took shape under the influence of Mediterranean hellenistic culture. That culture was grounded in what she calls "alienated consciousness," an outlook characterized by men's rejection of their own bodiliness, their fear of women's bodies, and human aspiration to spiritual or angelic existence.[28] The cultural bias that matter is at best a necessary evil which religion could teach us to transcend has persisted into the twentieth century, even in a church which proclaims that God took flesh and dwells among us.

In this collection Craighead the contemplative offers us the fruit of a lifetime spent beyond that aspiration for the angelic life. With the gift of awareness she calls her "subterranean" source, she plants us firmly back on the earth, and invites us into the mystery of the female body. She finds both earth and body to be good and the dwelling place of the God whose face we seek.

As I read her account of a dream she had shortly after her mother's death, I recalled Teresa of Avila's account of *The Interior Castle,* and was moved to reflect on the difference. I cannot put Craighead's dream painting into words; I can report her story of the experience behind the painting.

In the dream her grandfather, a Rock Island trainman, took her and her grandmother for an extraordinary locomotive ride. The train moved into a strange landscape, an egg-shaped planet suspended in space. They rode to the interior of the planet, moving through caverns and tunnels whose walls were shining jewels from which a sensation of sweetness came. She heard people chanting words that echoed the book of Revelation: "The walls are ornate with precious stones of every sort: the first is dark green jasper . . . the ninth yellow topaz . . . the twelfth violet amethyst. . . ." Then she recognizes where she is. "I realize that my grandparents are carrying me through the maze of my mother's body." Then they reach the innermost grotto, Grandpa announces the destination: "Lodestone." Her grandmother calls out "Motherlode."[29]

That narrative resonates with Teresa of Avila's imagery. In the opening lines of *The Interior Castle* she tells us, ". . . we consider our soul to be like a castle made entirely out of diamonds or very clear crystal, in which there are many rooms, just as in heaven there are many dwelling places."[30] Two obvious similarities appear in the two accounts of deepest reality, the many connected inner spaces and the jewels manifesting the splendor of these spaces. But there is a telling difference. Teresa's controlling image is architectural—a mansion. Meinrad Craighead's is biological—the inner recesses of the female body. In comparing the two images I found what has long been troublesome for me even in as attractive a spiritual writer as Teresa.

Teresa of Avila uses the images of the spiritual tradition as that tradition has come to her, alienated from the body. To enter the realm she invites me to consider, I have to make two imaginative leaps which distance me from myself. First, I have to locate myself in my "soul," a realm which eludes my mundane experience of my being. Then I have to imagine my elusive soul as

27

a complex building whose architecture I must master in order to locate what I am looking for. Until Craighead offered the alternative image to me, I had not recognized how distancing the traditional image was, presuming rather that the problem was my fragile hold on spiritual experience. How much simpler to know with certainty that the journey toward God is like a movement through the many openings into the recesses of our body, into the dark center where life ebbs and flows. There we can find the mystery hidden for all ages but present for those who know how to see, for those who know how to hear the voice speaking within.

ALIENATION: A POET SEEKING GOD

The poet Anne Sexton was a contemplative woman and a God-seeker. Unlike the artist Meinrad Craighead in whom affirming images of the earth and body lived from early childhood, Sexton was burdened by the alienated consciousness which burdens the whole of western civilization. Her collection of thirty-nine poems, *The Awful Rowing Toward God,* recounts her effort to move against the current, to resist the tide, to escape the undertow of personal and communal alienation from one's own human being which in turn

distances us from God. In the opening poem she
speaks of a child's life

> with its cruel houses
> and people who seldom touched—
> though touch is all—[31]

She recalls

> the nagging rain, the sun turning into poison
> and all of that, saws working through my
>   heart. . . .

Nevertheless, she grew up, doing things women
must do:

> I wore rubies and bought tomatoes
> and now, in my middle age,
> about nineteen in the head, I'd say,
> I am rowing, I am rowing. . . .

She expresses confidence that God somehow lies
ahead of her,

> like an island I had not rowed to.

When she arrives she anticipates divine healing:

> I will get rid of the rat inside of me,
> the gnawing pestilential rat.

God will take it with his two hands
and embrace it.

In the concluding poem, Anne Sexton foresees
reaching her destination,

mooring my rowboat
at the dock of the island called God.[32]

She arrives

with blisters that broke and healed
and broke and healed—
saving themselves over and over.

The meeting turns into a quick poker game
where she wins and God wins, something made
possible because

A wild card had been announced
but I had not heard it. . . .

In the end, the two, God and Anne, join in riot-
ous, joyous laughter, and she declares:

I . . .
love you so for your wild card . . .
and lucky love.

The salvation Anne Sexton anticipates in
this pair of poems will come from an alien and

not an inner source. We can recognize in her ex-
pectation the dominant images of the biblical
texts, underscored by her report that the dock at
which she moors on the island called God is fish-
shaped. With full Catholic sensibility, she alludes
to the early Christian designation of Christ as
fish, the concealing in the Greek anagram I-C-
Th-U-S the acclamation, "Jesus Christ, Son of
God and Savior!"

The rest of the collection shows Anne
searching for God through a strenuous journey
to escape from herself. Why? Because her inward
probings too often reveal filth and decay. She
confesses that she had killed her own heart because she once named it EVIL.[33] Her absence of
self-worth and her self-disgust ultimately lead
her to suicide not many years after the publica-
tion of this collection. Before she takes that step,
she seeks the help of wise men everywhere.

Characterizing herself as "The Poet of Ignorance," she asserts that she does not know the
truth about the earth, the moon, the stars, and
God. She does know one truth:

> . . . I have a body
> and I cannot escape from it. . . .
> It is written on the table of destiny
> that I am stuck here in human form.[34]

Accepting that fact, she asks for help with her
basic problem:

> There is an animal inside me,
> clutching fast to my heart,
> a huge crab.

She has sought medical advice, but the doctors of Boston "have thrown up their hands." She had tried to go about her business, ignoring the clutching pain around her heart. She had tried prayer:

> but as I pray the crab grips harder
> and the pain enlarges.

The only relief comes from a dream she has. Of the dream she says simply that perhaps

> the crab was my ignorance of God.

Even of that she cannot be sure:

> But who am I to believe in dreams?

Anne Sexton knew something of God the Mother in her awful rowing. She speaks of

> the salt of God's belly
> where I floated in a cup of darkness.[35]

If her memory of that place is dim, it is because

32

> . . . the light of the kitchen
> gets in the way.

Still, she recalls,

> . . . there was a dance
> when I kneaded the bread
> there was a song my mother used to sing.

If the sharpest God images Anne knows are male, she nevertheless also believes that God's existence is as alienated as hers.

> God loafs around heaven,
> without a shape
> but He would like to smoke His cigar
> and bite his fingernails.
> God owns heaven
> but He craves the earth . . .
> . . . most of all he envies bodies,
> He who has no body. . . .
> He does not envy the soul so much.
> He is all soul
> but he would like to have it in a body
> and come down
> and give it a bath
> now and then.[36]

Not surprisingly, the images clustering here are those we have found before in Teresa of Avila and Meinrad Craighead—souls and bodies, heaven and earth, the dwelling place of God. But we get a third configuration with Anne Sexton. She thinks God finds the ghostly realm to which he is eternally banished as uncongenial as she finds it.

Ambivalence characterizes Anne's experience of the God search. As she looks into being human on this earth she suffers massive mood swings and records the full arc in her poems. On one occasion Anne, "the God-Monger," goes off in search of answers about the other world. She went looking for "animal wisdom" and met a mouse who pushed three things toward her as gifts: a gourd of water, a gourd of beer, and a dish of gravy. It was not what she thought she needed, she reports, describing her soul "as a clothes closet of dresses that did not fit."[37] But "these simply had to be enough," she remarks, and then asks, "Who am I to reject the naming of food in a time of famine?"

In another moment she can deny the importance of life's ordinary gifts and recognize she is still looking for the mystery of God in the wrong places. She writes:

> I cannot walk an inch
> without trying to walk to God.
> I cannot move a finger
> without trying to touch God.[38]

But of course the situation is that she does not know the right place. She names long lists of places she has walked and of things she has touched only to hear heaven reply, "Not so! Not so!" "Where then?" she asks. The answer comes,

> Look to your heart
> that flutters in and out like a moth.
> God is not indifferent to your need.
> You have a thousand prayers,
> but God has one.

The answer is a cruel joke on Anne, for she has already told us that her heart is crabbed with unrelieved pain which only the unknown God can heal. Furthermore, she has already pronounced her own heart "Evil." That finally is the tragedy of Anne Sexton's passionate lifelong rowing. Alienation from her own being distances her from the God at her center.

In contrast with the stability, security, and tranquillity Meinrad Craighead experiences because of her grounding in the soil of the earth and in her own female body—both images for her of God the Mother—Anne Sexton is cut adrift. She struggled courageously but unsuccessfully with life's terror.

REVELATION:
THE NAMING OF THE UNFATHOMABLE

Awareness of life's terror is also in evidence in the writings of the third woman we want to take note of, Annie Dillard. For the contemplative Dillard the terrors are themselves invitations to venture closer to look upon the face of God.

Where do God-seekers typically look for God? Anne Sexton professed her ignorance and looked everywhere. Meinrad Craighead invited us "to the edge of the central opening," imaged in the dark recesses of the earth and our own female bodies. The feminist liturgists summon us monthly to Miriam's well. Annie Dillard images the dwelling place of God at the outermost edges of human experience, symbolized in the poles at the farthest reaches of all culture and civilization, but experienced in life's incomprehensible events.

Dillard's own contemplative journey as she has recorded it in her published essays seems to have begun in her fascination with the world of nature.[39] What fascinates her is not only nature's design but especially its randomness, terror, and violence. Careful attentiveness to the world of weasels and eagles, pond scum, genetics and geography reveals the mystery of life as both compelling and fearsome.

With a contemplative awareness that the divine presence will overwhelm those who draw near, Annie Dillard has remarked tellingly on the surface meetings with God that characterize church assemblies. She speaks of the "set pieces of liturgy" as "certain words which people have successfully addressed to God without their getting killed."[40] She writes,

> On the whole, I do not find Christians, outside of the catacombs, sufficiently sensible of conditions. Does anyone have the foggiest idea of what sort of power we so blithely invoke? Or, as I suspect, does no one believe a word of it? The churches are children playing on the floor with their chemistry sets, mixing up a batch of TNT to kill a Sunday morning. It is madness to wear ladies . . . hats to church; we should all be wearing crash helmets; they should lash us to our pews. For the sleeping God may wake someday and take offence, or the waking God may draw us out to where we can never return.[41]

Dillard is not rejecting liturgical worship. This passage occurs in a context in which she reports that she has become Roman Catholic. Her assertion is that the life of prayer is more demanding than going to church leads us to believe.

The pull of God has regularly drawn Annie Dillard into solitude. She narrates how in one period of her life she took up residence on an island in northern Puget Sound in Washington State. "I came to study hard things—rock mountains and salt sea—and to temper my spirit on their edges." Her prayer was, "Teach me thy ways, O Lord." She recognizes the prayer is "rash . . . and one I cannot but recommend."[42] As Dillard tells her story, the prayer sequel was absurd. In its simplest lines, the story is this. A local child she has met and played with just once—their faces were alike she had observed—sets off with her father in a light plane. The plane crashed; "the fuel exploded; and Julie Norwich seven years old burnt off her face."[43] What does this absurdity mean? "You wake up and a plane falls out of the sky. . . . Ashes, ashes, all fall down. How could I have forgotten?" she wonders.[44]

Dillard had come to her northern Pacific solitude to read classical mystical literature. Reading now, against the backdrop of the plane's fall from the sky, she finds that what the mystics write can make sense only if it speaks to Julie Norwich's condition. And she knows that Julie Norwich's absurd child's existence speaks tellingly of what she calls "God's tooth." Annie Dillard reads that God wants us to risk meeting reality beyond our images and ideas. Hearing from the mystics that "God despises ideas"—all human effort to put order into life's experience—she wonders, "God

38

despises everything, apparently."[45] But she presses to understand the dark absurdity.

Meditating the texts of the mystics and the text of Julie Norwich's life she pronounces, "The god of today is a glacier."[46] Humans dwell in the shifting glacial crevasses, unheard, but crushed by the glacial stirrings. She recalls the gospel question, "Who sinned? This blind man or his parents?" And she hears the two-pronged answer: No one sinned. The works of God are being made manifest in him (Jn 9:1–41). And Annie Dillard is caught short. God manifested in innocent victims? "Do we really need more victims to remind us we're all victims?"

She knows the answer is yes. "Yes, in fact we do. We do need reminding, not of what God can do, but of what he cannot do, or will not, which is to catch time in its free fall and stick a nickel's worth of sense into our days."[47]

Absurdity is not life's anomaly; absurdity prevails. "We are most deeply asleep at the switch," writes Annie Dillard, "when we fancy we control any switches at all." When we finally awake to reality beyond life's illusions, we will no longer need to force events to make sense. The only events in any lifetime, says Dillard, "are thoughts, the heart's hard turning and the heart's slow learning where to love and whom."[48]

On what solid ground can anyone stand if we

are really free-falling through our lifetimes? Julie Norwich lies in a hospital bed with her face burnt off. Annie Dillard is forced to look again at the hard things she came to understand, on which she wanted to temper her spirit. She remembers an off-beat medieval vision of this world's reality in all its dullness and hardness. More base, more fundamental than mineral salts and earth and rock, this substrata of reality is in touch with the Absolute. Its immanence in the material transcends everything it undergirds. The medievals called this invisible transcendent substance "Holy the Firm."[49] Even the meanest of hard things rests in its divine realm; nothing, however base, is cut off from it.

Julie Norwich, face blazing, is a chosen messenger of God's presence. In a manner more terrifying than that of Isaiah the prophet (Is 6:1–10), Julie is called to announce with her life, "Holy! Holy! Holy!" inviting onlookers and listeners to contemplate hard, incomprehensible love.

The world has two kinds of nuns, says Dillard, in the light of her meeting with the God revealed through Julie. There are those inside and those outside convents. Whichever kind she is, the nun's vocation is contemplation of the real. Dillard's dangerous prayer for Julie is "Live." Then she makes her promise, "I'll be the nun for you. I am now."[50]

40

Dillard's experiences of God in consuming flame and crushing glacial ice are certainly less welcoming than those images which the artist Meinrad Craighead shows us of God present in warm earth, moon, light, water and the inner recesses of our being. We know that such imaginative insight with its terrifying message of God's love is capable of overwhelming us, precisely as Monica Furlong warned.

When Jesus of Nazareth faced the terror of God's love on Calvary in an historical moment, he was showing humankind the same mysterious love that Annie Dillard recognized in the innocent victim Julie Norwich. But the church places a protective shield around life's ordinary terror, teaching us to gaze on Jesus, when we might well have been journeying through the Word of God Jesus Christ, naming our own experiences, on the path of the journey toward an incomprehensible, unfathomable God. Unlike routine churchgoers, Annie Dillard has had eyes to see into her own experiences of life and a listening to receive the word of God's self-disclosure. Annie Dillard, who knows both Jesus and Julie, can cry "Holy, holy, holy!" wherever she walks on the surface of the earth.

Meinrad Craighead and Annie Dillard share the insight that the world of ordinary things in time's free fall is revelatory of God. The salvation history of the biblical narrative is not the only bearer of God's self-disclosure. This conviction does not negate the written texts of the biblical revelation. It invites us to see more. It invites us to understand that the word of God speaking to the ear of the human heart sounds everywhere.

HEARTFELT RESISTANCE— HEARTFELT LISTENING: A CONCLUSION

The gift of female human being may be to be more attuned to the word within creation because the creating God has made the female, like the ocean tides, responsive to the pull of the moon and given her ease with nature's dark places. Western religious institutions, from the days of Moses to our own, have not yet been able to receive women's spiritual wisdom and to celebrate it. We can only speculate on the reason for the church's refusal of this gift.

The church as we know it is an historical reality, a religious institution whose membership is male and female but whose gate-keepers, shapers, and guardians of the tradition are all males. Yet it is not inevitable that men's shaping of the tradition must draw almost exclusively on andro-centric images. As Adrienne Rich has noted, "The one unifying, incontrovertible experience shared by all women and all men is that months-long period we spent unfolding inside a woman's body. All human life on the planet is born of woman."[51]

Why then does the church of Jesus Christ ignore or negate as inauthentic God imagery this universal experience of being enveloped in maternal mystery? Meinrad Craighead has painted her experiences of this feminine God as her origin and destiny, on the journey from the womb to the tomb in the recesses of the earth. What is the terror here which leads to ecclesiastical rejection of this universal experience as revelatory of divine saving presence? What fear transforms this experience into a diminished, controllable image of an enigmatically human Mary who is the Mother of Jesus and yet somehow the Mother of the race?

Only males can enter within themselves and try to name whatever terror is latent in such a revelation. But Rich suggests one possible explanation—that males are "haunted by the force of the idea of *dependence on a woman for life itself.*"[52] In any case, we must dare to ask what insight the church is refusing when it refuses the female as a source of orthodox symbols of divine presence.[53]

Wisdom not received, wisdom neglected, becomes wisdom of dubious worth, finally no wisdom at all. Too many women long ago stopped believing in the worth of the gift they have. They stopped listening for the inner word of divine

43

mystery trying to find its voice through them. Now, within these past two decades many women have begun growing in their capacity to hear the word and to recognize the embrace of divine love in their lives. But too many women are still voiceless about spiritual matters. No longer deaf to the word spoken in inner stillness, such women remain mute, unable to talk about what they have heard.

In any given culture or epoch, only a few people, men or women, have the skills to craft words and to shape images in ways that the rest of us can recognize as the truth of our own inner experience. That pair of qualities, openness to inner experience combined with uncommon skills for writing or painting, was decisive for my choice of Annie Dillard, Anne Sexton, and Meinrad Craighead as exemplars of contemporary women at prayer.

Mystics who are also poets and artists are the therapists of the imagination the church needs today. Their creativity gives us a language for communication. Receiving their gifts we have the opportunity for recognition: "Aha! I've been there, too," or "Oh, yes, I see, I know," or "No, I've not met flame and ice in my own journey into God, but I trust I will not be annihilated when I do."

On the other hand many churchgoers may be blinded by these unfamiliar visions of the living God or deaf to this new ecstatic speech. These seeming impediments are an indirect invitation to let go for a while of the God we are clinging to, whether for comfort or in anger. Unless the churches have some predisposition to inner silence and detachment from all the familiar images of God, some of us will get stuck permanently, while others become increasingly alienated. The gap will grow between our life experience and our God language. We will mistrust what life itself teaches, or we will become godless because the god of the church of Jesus Christ does not speak to our human hearts.

Feminist mystics have the courage to abandon the security and safety of what we all already claim to know about God and to respond as solitary voyagers to the divine summons to come nearer. Feminist liturgists, more daring than ecclesiastical liturgists, gather together at "the edge of the central opening" to move into unknown darkness secured and anchored to one another, rappellers ready to break each other's falls and to celebrate each other's recoveries. The churches should be cheering them on, waiting expectantly for their reports.

Does it really matter that men and women have mutually respectful words to speak to one another about God when we gather for prayer? Most certainly it does matter. It is the whole church which has a call to contemplative living, to seek the face of God and to worship in spirit and in truth. Christian contemplatives make the journey "up the path of speech." All true contemplatives begin the journey with the pious intention of seeking God, but the great discovery of the journey is that on the way we find ourselves. For in the beginning, before we lost our way, we were created male and female as God's images.

1. Gregory the Great, *The Dialogues*. Book II.
2. Translated selections from most of these writers can be found in *Medieval Women's Visionary Literature*, ed. Elizabeth A. Petroff. New York: Oxford U. Press, 1986.
3. See, for example, *Women's Spirituality*, Joann Wolski Conn, ed. New York: Paulist Press, 1986.
4. Teresa of Avila comments often on nuns' problems with male confessors. See, for example, *The Way of Perfection*, Ch 5.3. *The Collected Works of St. Teresa of Avila*, Vol II. Tr. Kieran Kavanaugh and Otilio Rodriguez. Washington, DC: ICS Publications, 1980. Margery Kempe gives a vivid account of the second problem in *The Book of Margery Kempe*, tr. Susan Dickman, in Petroff, ed., 321ff.
5. Thomas Aquinas, *Summa Theologica*. Supplement Q39, A.1.
6. "The Revelations of St. Gertrude the Great," part II, in Petroff, ed., 222–231.
7. A popular account and further documentation is given in my essay "Devotions and Renewal Movements," in *Called to Prayer*. Collegeville, MN: The Liturgical Press, 1986, 49–54.
8. Meinrad Craighead, *The Mother's Songs. Im-*

ages of God the Mother. Mahwah, NJ: Paulist Press, 1986, 15, 59; Penina V. Adelman, *Miriam's Well.* Fresh Meadows, NY: Biblio Press, 1986.

9. Annie Dillard, *Teaching a Stone to Talk. Expeditions and Encounters.* New York: Harper and Row, 1982. "An Expedition to the Pole," 17–52.

10. Sandra Schneiders, *Women and the Word. The Gender of God in the New Testament and the Spirituality of Women.* Mahwah, NJ: Paulist Press, 1986, 70–71.

11. Mary Collins, "Obstacles to Liturgical Creativity," in M. Collins and D. Power, ed. *Liturgy: A Creative Tradition* (Concilium 162). Edinburgh: T & T Clark, 1983, 19–26.

12. Gail Ramshaw Schmidt, *Christ in Sacred Speech.* Philadelphia: Fortress Press, 1986, 10.

13. Jean Leclercq, *The Love of Learning and the Desire for God.* New York: Mentor Omega Books, 1962, 21–32, 76–93.

14. Monica Furlong, *Contemplating Now.* Cambridge, MA: Cowley Publications, 1986. Reprint of Westminster Press ed., 1971, 36.

15. Christian women's groups have done similar explorations. Among some such groups the gospel account of the Samaritan woman at the well provides a gathering center. For one account of Christian feminist liturgies see

Rosemary Ruether, *Woman Church*, San Francisco: Harper and Row, 1985.

16. Adelman, 8–14.
17. Adelman, 63–64.
18. Adelman, 12ff.
19. Victor W. Turner, *Forms of Symbolic Action.* Seattle: University of Washington Press, 1969.
20. Adelman, 43.
21. Susanne Langer, *Philosophy in a New Key. A Study of the Symbolism of Reason, Rite, and Art.* NY: Mentor Books, 1942, 136ff.
22. Craighead, "Introduction," n.p.
23. Craighead, "Hallower," 18–19.
24. Craighead, "Vessel," 66–67.
25. Craighead, "Wind," 64–65.
26. Craighead, "Her Face," 1.
27. A brief exploration of this matter from the standpoint of liturgical history is offered in Collins, "Devotions," 60–67.
28. Rosemary Ruether, "Misogynism and Virginal Feminism in the Fathers of the Church," in Ruether, ed., *Sexism and Religion.* New York: Simon and Schuster, 1974, 150–83.
29. Craighead, "Night," 60–61.
30. *The Interior Castle,* in *Collected Works,* Vol II, Ch 1.1.
31. Anne Sexton, *The Awful Rowing Toward God.* Boston: Houghton, Mifflin Co., 1975. Ref-

erence to a specific poem will be made at the first of any series of citations. "Rowing," 1–2.

32. Sexton, "The Rowing Endeth," 85–86.
33. Sexton, "The Dead Heart," 36–37.
34. Sexton, "The Poet of Ignorance," 28–29.
35. Sexton, "The Fish That Walked," 20–21.
36. Sexton, "The Earth," 24–25.
37. Sexton, "The God-Monger," 62.
38. Sexton, "Not So. Not So," 83–84.
39. Annie Dillard, *Pilgrim at Tinker Creek*. San Francisco: Harper and Row, 1974; *Holy the Firm*, 1977; *Teaching a Stone to Talk*, 1982.
40. Dillard, *Holy,* 59.
41. Dillard, *Teaching,* 40–41.
42. Dillard, *Holy,* 19.
43. Dillard, *Holy,* 36.
44. Dillard, *Holy,* 42–43.
45. Dillard, *Holy,* 45.
46. Dillard, *Holy,* 49.
47. Dillard, *Holy,* 60.
48. Dillard, *Holy,* 62.
49. Dillard, *Holy,* 68–70.
50. Dillard, *Holy,* 74–76.
51. Adrienne Rich, *Of Woman Born*. New York: W. W. Norton & Co., 1976, 11.
52. Rich, 11. Emphasis in the original.
53. See Bernard Lonergan, *Insight*. San Francisco: Harper and Row, 1957, 187–94, for a discussion of avoidance of insight through the repression of images.

MARY COLLINS, O.S.B., Ph.D., is associate professor of liturgical studies in the Department of Religion and Religious Education at the Catholic University of America, Washington, D.C. She has been a Benedictine Sister of Atchison, Kansas, since 1957. An author, editor and lecturer, she is past president of both the North American Academy of Liturgy and the North American Liturgical Conference and is associate director of the Center for Benedictine Studies in Atchison.